D0567164

3
HARRIS COUNTY PUBLIC LIBRARY

811.6 Cou
Coultas, Brenda
The tatters

$22.95
ocn861335333
04/10/2014

WITHDRAWN

THE TATTERS

WESLEYAN POETRY

the tatters

BRENDA COULTAS

WESLEYAN UNIVERSITY PRESS | MIDDLETOWN, CONNECTICUT

Wesleyan University Press

Middletown CT 06459

www.wesleyan.edu/wespress

© 2014 Brenda Coultas

All rights reserved

Manufactured in the United States of America

Designed by Mindy Basinger Hill

Typeset in Parkinson Electra Pro

Wesleyan University Press is a member of the Green
Press Initiative. The paper used in this book meets their
minimum requirement for recycled paper.

Library of Congress Cataloging-in-Publication Data

Coultas, Brenda.
[Poems. Selections]
The tatters / Brenda Coultas.
      pages   cm.
ISBN 978-0-8195-7419-0 (cloth : alk. paper)
(Wesleyan Poetry Series)
I. Title.
PS3603.O886A6 2014
811'.6—dc23

5   4   3   2   1

DEDICATED TO THE MEMORY OF BRAD WILL

Brad Will was a poet, Indymedia journalist, anarchist, and
a friend of mine. He was murdered in Oaxaca, Mexico, on
October 27, 2006, while filming a street battle between the
Oaxaca governor Ulises Ruiz Ortiz's thugs and APPO, the
Popular Assembly of the People, during a months-long teachers'
strike in which at least eleven were killed. For more information:
www.friendsofbradwill.org.

CONTENTS

THE TATTERS

MY TREE

I found a pearl and wore it in my ear
Deep ocean echoes sing like a seashell

A girl promised a purse filled with jewels, if I would be her friend
Purses open secrets as priceless as pills in a jeweled box

Loose pearls, enough to imagine what a great loss that necklace was or
was not

I like to see metal turn red and glow and to hear its hiss when it meets
the water. Leather bellows, suspended from the ceiling, pump air into
the fire. Long-handled tongs and picks forge mostly nails. I open all the
old purses. There might be change left in one.

I built you a tree of light to see by
To listen to digital libraries in your palm.
Renamed myself writing this book, renamed myself after building
this tree

I burnt candles all night to grow these leaves.

I fed books to the flame, to make a blaze to read by
Mined libraries to power this tower of light

Built sparkling branches
with flaming pages for leaves
dense as the weeping willow's cascade of curls

On the mountain ridge my tree stands head and shoulders above
the hardwoods. Along the roadway wooden poles, bathed in chemicals,
hold up a network of wire

I built a tree, more cell than sweeping pine or black walnut, as natural
as pink pine needles or a silver holiday tree. Glittery pine boughs glue-
gunned on

No needles on the floor
No forest smell

My gift is glittery and eternal
even in synthetic shreds
dumped on a landlocked city sidewalk
it finds its way to the sea

A MASS FOR BRAD WILL

If I were a quill I'd write in bright feathers all about you bursting
into flight over the heads of cops

If I were a handsome feather, I'd walk to City Hall
in full plumage and release all of Manhattan's political prisoners

If I were a quill I'd give you life
on this quiet page

On a four feather day, last one ruffled
another grey with black-banded top

Then pinfeathers
regroup to make a full on . . .

You might think his body was blown to bits
or burned to ashes

Thrown into a favorite body of water
Maybe one of the great lakes

You might think he was made of feathers or of bird weight
No, he was buried whole, perhaps with bullets intact.

Critical mass. Yes, he liked to say it.

Critical mass is a beautiful way to say we gather
to shut down the system
so bicyclists can take over the streets

Critical mass
a way to say we gather
so that it matters

When the bicyclists take over the streets
and bring the city
to a standstill, Brad said that
is critical mass

I asked, "What happens when the city is shut down?"
He said, "Then we'll dance."

He liked a song about a drop of water. In this song, the drops
came together to form a trickle, then a stream, a river, a body of
water, the power of the water made us aware that we belonged to
the earth, that we would protect her, and by the end of the song,
the river was free.

THE MIDDEN

Blue stone quarries
stone of touch
stone marker or the stone left behind
shell middens and clay pipes and passenger pigeons dressed in blues
the stone that gazes heaven side up
the day which is red and pink corners

Burnish the blue stone & quarry the earth
dynamite time

Perfection is time's work or what makes bluestone blue or what makes
a quartz crystal

Halo surrounds —— core of labyrinth ——— glow departs from an
ember

Opposing fire & fetching cool petals
quietly foxed or bat claw unhinged
cut from mussel shell or bone
buttons lie underground

Walking through coals into a city within the fire
entering the ember, encased in a protective suit
to bring out handfuls of what that world inside burning wood is like

Flame in the air, gas fields full of devil's spit
yellow eye of methane

When the flame is in the air and the night is eye & thigh high
paper laid on an ember browns then flames

Walking inside the flame, or an ember of heated talk opening doors
poured from the long-necked bucket or dug from a shallow seam

Standing in the doorway of an ember
the door is a passage that my friend leaves ajar

Walking through embers: a marriage with its pleasures of heat and light
and the pain of heat and light
stoking the fire inside

Oil pumps in a corn field
Satan's fires
burn off the methane

Freestanding coal shack & packed trailer parks of burning coals
overflow the double-wide with its cathedral ceilings, whirlpool tubs,
and master suites

The landfill handed me a ball of paper, a washed-out small boulder of
print. I cracked it open and read "Danny Kaye performing live." And I
thought, How long has he been dead?

Like the midden of books and papers stacked by the bed, make of it
what you will. I put my rage on top to cultivate later, the midden of
paper and print, headlines and ink, mixed pulp from long ago industrial
and urban waste will topple and release a flood of ivory and soft grays
and blacks

Dust tops the PC, dot matrix printer, and typewriter in a thrift shop
The Apple in the barn is boxy and hard
Cords long gone
Plastic phones turn a palm into light

The inside awash with take-out containers—driver's seat cleared
of—— cigarette butts, newspapers, plastic forks, spoons, and knives
ready to go

The captain's logbook was inked heavy with stamps. I ask the long-
dead captain, Is it like a wax cylinder or like tree rings or like grooves
set in foil? Is it Thomas Edison's talking machine or Bell's telephone?
Is it an echo chamber of the ocean or a talking drum?

There were the sounds that I couldn't carve, the blood I couldn't catch, dust fell, sprinkling itself over the glass cases of artifacts, over baleen piano keys, carved dice, combs, and mirrors. In his log book I silently entered how the whale's eardrums are as large as a child's head (how each is painted with a frisky portrait of a man and a woman.)

I carve an animal into the logbook, cutting through a hundred pages of sea notes, of sightings, of oil harvested and rendered. I cut through accounts of the sperm whale's death throes, of harpooners who froze as they closed in on the chase. With my pen, I carve another animal into the book. A tooth out of a tusk. Baleen into corset stays. Press breasts and penises into bone, I make fine canes for gentlemen.

Underneath the childhood clothing, grade school valentines, and schoolbooks my mother stored in a trunk, what shows? An arm? Toe? I like to stick my feet out. What gives my presence away? A rumpled sheet under the blanket? A barely perceptible ripple.

Sitting perched on letters and newspapers, under the mattress, tables, and on chairs and inside shoe boxes

Bread box
Of the other books
Leaf press
Prayer-card holder
Toast tray

I store neatly pressed handkerchiefs and hand fans embossed with bible verses and funeral home ads inside an encyclopedia

Press a green spider into the book, cross-eyed and alive and already very flat

Press in a dream of living in the deep blue of space, like the planet earth. The earth, an eyeball of the galaxy

Press in deep blue space, a blue ball of light rotating through the black inky void around a larger system, a bigger star, a blue milky marble, moving.—Out of an ember cooling and firing again—gravity of milky puppy breath—milky marble home.

ANIMATIONS

Coloring the glass with pee or peering at a blue dense enough to be alive or to influence a human or inhuman action, the feather death crown is a spiral, and in automatic writing, the spirals grow smaller and smaller before any actual communication.

Spiral, a tornado wind in the pen and on the page

Pressed glass hen on nest
girls in frosted petticoats
white darning eggs
clear radio tubes
cobalt eyewash cup talks of sand and heat
speaks of tinctures and rubs soothing as a salve or as beauty
the sand grains talk of rock and water

The feather crowns say, "There must be a better way to signify heaven or salvation." Those who gather crowns keep them under glass or in their best candy boxes and pass them on as evidence of afterlife.

This one gathers the living. The feathers having chosen a spokes-one. Earth shaken, pressed glass pink in permanent petticoats. Arms pinned. Returning items to the sea and beads to the wire. Pushing horseshoe crabs back into time in hopes of reanimation.

Meteorite in a field of pussy willows
Rose crystal skull abandoned on a city sidewalk

Bottles swim into the sea, gather mass, and offer a lift, a flotilla
for drifting hitchhikers. A spoon lifts cereal from the cranial bowl of a
medical school skull.

A fossil is a fiction written by time.

Elephants bearing salt and pepper, trunks tied to the pony's back.
Unyielding, brittle, and easy to snap, the bridled pony, bribed or beaten
to walk at night, over canyons and valleys of green sleep, laden with
packages, tied tightly with red string, yet some fall and shatter as if
they'd arrived by post. Biscuit boxes and camping stoves are small, but
heavy like stone houses.

Moving through woods, toward the big deep fragment of an enameled
bucket. Depression pink tongue tip, thick and scalloped, radiates from
the car in the woods. Hubcap pain-spokes outward from the center.

While sleeping in the woods, a matchbox cemetery turns to stone
over time.

Shards of mirror given as a gift. Busty angel holds a dove aloft in her
hands. Oyster shell middens replace teeth as eternal as the ball of
a titanium hip. What remains is a pewter vessel, hard and grey, that
serves better as a pencil cup than as a grog glass.

A GAZE

"Shale is incredibly complex. When it comes to finding
the shale sweet spot and unlocking it in a cost-efficient manner,
no one has more experience than Halliburton."
Halliburton website

I

A man texts a photograph of his meal, but to who? Himself or others?
Others too, texting in a crowd on 1st Avenue as glaciers recede.
They do not feel the fading cold of the ice. Only the heat of the
key strokes.

A man texts crystal water glass pixels to quench real thirst.

I texted forward a rumor of siphoned great lakes water to China. A
Chinese bureaucrat texts images of fresh lake water to billions at home.

At the top of a mountain, where only small mammals live, the air
is thin and gives me panic. I do not belong above the tree line even
though I can drive there. Stopping to send a pic of the lichen sponge by
the gift shop on the glacier, the phone lens: an extension of my eyes.

At times, I forget that I am not an extension of the machine until I
burn my palms touching a hot metal pot: recoil and remember to use
hot pads to protect the flesh fabric that covers the hand bones.

From the glacier tops, bodies of mountain climbers in the dead zone. Will their corpses sweeten or embitter the waters of the Ganges?

The leather shoes of the ice man texted forward.

Sometimes, the tap runs while I brush my teeth and empty bathwater down the drain.

The last glass of water sits before you, how fast or slow will you drink it?

We load the car on Highway 50, the loneliest highway in the USA. It winds through Nevada crossing the Pony Express route and ancient seabeds. Crinoid stems thirst for the ancient sea.

Last glass of glacier water boils in the kettle. Saffron threads of a Viking beard cloud the water glass.

Theft of water, relocation, diverted from its bed. Hydro-fracking. I never thought they'd use our water against us.

When we began with this full jug of water without thinking until the police chased us away from the creek of who owns the water. Or that satellite overhead, branded by a private owner over public space.

Wanted to absorb it, to get to the bottom and start all over again. A great anxiety about finishing and throwing it away, with an inch still in the bottom, the backwash.

Who owns the creeks and waterways of this valley? The only legal course is midstream so that anglers can trout fish without trespass.

Into the last glass, I stir the reindeer scat with a herding stick captured from the thaw.

The water is an hourglass, and I write fast as I can before it runs dry.

A glass of water from last glacier sits before you on the table, you gaze at the logo of an abundant flowing stream or the name of the spring which somehow sounds pure and far away as an iceberg, calved off and lassoed from the warming world. Even though you know the source is a corporate tap of public water.

Fertilizer runs off into our family well. I used to picture a whale, a Moby Dick under the cornfield, a leviathan as the source of our water because only a vessel the size of a sperm whale could contain the water that flowed on command from the tap. Even though people spoke of the well running dry, ours magically replenished itself under the blanket of Monsanto crops.

The last glass of water sits before you, will you drink it slowly savoring the taste of the glacier?

It flows on the green logo and facsimile of a mountain stream of abundant water.

"Natural" is highlighted and in a yellow circle it is written, "contains 16 servings" and there are only two of us left since this now nearly empty jug was opened.

We might have swum to our seats in the crystal underground cavern or inside the whale. The water table is a banquette of the last supper, the clear plates as detailed as a sea monkey's anatomy or the vulvas of Judy Chicago's dinner party.

A centerpiece of lilies welcomes us. A waiter comes with his crystal water pitcher, wrapped in white linen. He bows and we watch our glasses turn a cool blue anti-freeze shade.

Some harvest and sell the rights to rain. Although the water said clear and running and cool and unstoppable glacier tops and blue stones and slick rock and kill is Dutch for spring.

We have arrived at this point where a water source has become diamond-worthy. The vision withstands the weight of platters laden heavily with fruit and bread.

Gazing at water through glass prisms
Champagne with hollow stem
Turkish tea blue and silver panels
Crystal flute & jelly jar
Coil pot
Roman goblet
Ancient clay fragments of a water jug
Banana leaves
Cupped palms
Water rush
Flow of public and private
Locked website or paywall

We sit down before the guards can catch us.

Wastewater, its chemicals pass through the tablecloth, and infect it with radiation. Inside pantry doors, mining deep into the cabinet, the heavy minerals are stored in the far reaches of the cupboard and on the top shelf out of reach

Who holds the crystal-clear machine guns?
Who fires the shocks of the invisible fence?

We gaze at the fence of ownership
Once set for us
Then set against us

Taking shelter in the watershed, I thought, This is untouchable, such a treasure, Catskill pure. Taking shelter in a house that once sat in a place now underwater, a house meant to be drowned under the Ashokan. I sit in a dry chair before the woodburner.

Theft of water from Bishop Falls
Greatest heist of all
Starts the flow downstream.

Marcellus Shale sounds gendered and plentiful like the Roberta Tar Sands.
Shalenlaires, farmers made wealthy overnight, like Motown music.
Not like "stimulate" or "industrial wild."

Drinking in the morning dust of last evening's air
They use private forces against us
Weapons to keep us away from our water.

THE TATTERS

I

Cleanly folded paper lying in street
A job request for urine
I close my eyes
A broth of steaming piss

Transmission while walking briskly, slightly ruffled
Before bed, round butter cakes
After bed, devils' food
Bright red between sheets

On growing a perfect wing
I forgot about the purpose of flight or
cloak of a peacock

A wet pigeon said, "Why don't I ask for what I really want?"

I have forgotten the purpose
Of touching a child's hand
Of pigeon shit on perfect feathers
Of deep round cake pans

In taking it apart
to see how it works
I realized that I wish to control the means of production

Cast iron, pumped by muscle
pulleys and rope
(This I recognize as cast iron circle and hemp)
linens climb in and out the window

Rum-soaked cake
half eaten
on the table
to this we return

Dorothy Podber's belongings on the sidewalk. Charred wood,
even though that building was never on fire.

Diagrams of electrical machines. I like to look and don't care that
I don't understand.

I have lived a long time without knowing the names of the trees. Barely
able to recognize a locust leaf, and yet I can recognize the sight of oak,
even varnished or cobbled into a desk or plank. I have lived here, not
knowing that a rock dove is a pigeon. Of my apartment, knowing only
that the cockroaches are German and the rats Norwegian.

None of this is good and I worry about the scarcity of wood or if we
will ever have enough materials to reassemble the object after taking
it apart.

I took apart a hornet's nest after my brother had sprayed it with heavy
chemicals. In pursuit of the natural world, I cut a swath. A giant
lifting boards and logs, uncovering sleeping animals, or embryonic
mice. Worms, snakes, and salamanders all call me an asshole.

Today, cast iron cooking stove pulled up from the basement. Pinball
and bubblegum machine filled with crumbling candy.

Tonight, perhaps more of Dorothy Podber's belongings: a wooden
storage chest from below the street level, earthy and soft. The color
in the dark is dark. Caramel and full of the earth's products. Like the
rats who live below us, a night shade of dark, not rotten yet full of the
rot of newspapers, my contribution. I collect ephemera and revisit it
gleaning when I am alone making lists and piles by color or subject
or time.

Taking apart the nest, all in their beds of grey
I had to know and then I had nothing, clumps of paper, and the dead
in their paper beds. Hundreds and my brother was mad.
Yet this does not prevent me from asking what is inside the trunk on
the street? Picture postcards? Soft porn or hard sex toys?

Looking at the ground, the tatters of the nest I destroyed, but how
else could I know the nature of physical objects, and of my body?

I, a physical object, ask what's inside the body? A collection of
swallowed needles, fishhooks, and pennies.

For a long time looking in, gazing, trying to know the nature of the physical, like the man who could balance jagged sea rocks one on top another. He could know an object and if those boulders should be stacked as steady as plates or as delicately as a house of cards.

I, a physical object, reading *Anatomy*, 1924, colored plates, diagrams with overlays. It is good that I saved these thick books, each one a doorstopper on female anatomy and child care, from the time of paper and print, colored plates to lift and reveal. Each plate, like a candy pop, taking you further, dissolving layers until you reach the baby soft center.

Diagrams, like this one. See.

A man told me of finding the foot pedals of a sewing machine covered in dust on Mott Street, about how he put his foot to the pedal and the flywheel turned even though the rest of the machine was extinct.

Flywheel, I like to say it and see it

Alone with paper or reading from paper, in a room
It's quiet

Me, a noun, an animal from the time of the animals
I write and I eat with my hands

Working late and decoding secret writings from the tatters (read once of a wealthy young artist who slept in nests he made out of bedding in luxury hotel rooms. I thought a nest should be made of threads collected from the streets and should be humble like a quilt.)

The feather again (the blade). This time on the street. First quietly in
front, then as I move, cocks quietly to the 10 o'clock position. Later in
the day, silently soaked with winter salt
Too, same roach and rat
Regulars on the block

Can't recall the center, only the fury with which I tore it, then a drop in
the blood at realizing what I had done

Paper at my feet
Bodies
Stillborns
What little I know of other lives

I bought him a book of photographs of a hornet's nest, but is he satisfied? No. To please him I gather the pulp and piece it together with agitated human agency, I reconstruct hundreds of bedrooms for the young and old grey sleepers, I slipcover the common spaces of the hive. I coat the outside with paper-mache making this a very dark piñata. An insect house chewed into existence only to discover that he didn't want a nest, he wanted a trophy.

Intercepting messages barked out by Frank's box or the poems
of Hannah Weiner, and I follow my spirit guides Bernadette Mayer
and Brad Will

Bernadette is alive and owns many books and papers
Bernadette eats an egg at her writing desk every morning

I know Bernadette is alive because she leaves eggshells on her
writing desk

Brad is dead even though he used to eat fire

I have some of his objects which keep me from thoughts of his death
I lie
I have none of his objects, only a film of him breathing fire

Grandpa wrote his figures on panels of cigarette and candy cartons
and I saved their clutter too, even the phone numbers
I won't erase them thus keeping the Database of Phantoms alive

Wooden bowls feed me
Cup of tea makes me know I am alive
(If I were dead I could not feel the heat of the cup or taste the bitter
tannins)

Cup of tea distracts me from my death and the death of everyone I love
Bloodstained napkin told of toothache
Cup of tea said I was alive
Seedpods lay crushed on sidewalk

Rattan dining set told me to sit down and watch
Heavy coats and jackets feed the pigeons and squirrels
Chair legs ordered me to the desk, to write of this

No feathers today and "putting a meal on the table" is a
great distraction

An office chair facing a mound of garbage bags tried to get my
attention. Spirits of the chair and bags, and of the bus, hum on the
avenue and in the water fish sing the full glory of objects in the body.

Man said, "Delicious" as I walk by
Later on, a conversation with Rebecca over the problem of dinner
and care of food animals, including the winged bugs in the flour.

About the feathers
At my feet are feet
Even the homemade and humble
Dream of white beads

How can I read the banana skin with the neck pointed down and away?
Birds ignore me, cigarette butts refuse to make eye contact, I might be
dead after all.

If I can live long enough to know I can start my making. Then I will
really have something, like the man who mourned his dog. Until the
dog's ashes arrived, he felt incomplete.

Shaky since a child, I can thread a needle, but I cannot hold a
rifle steady

At the Five Points Mission, a bodega door, green and ajar, asks me to come in

Man on my stoop, cradles a pigeon. The bird is calm and the man is full of madness. I look closely at them, gleams of purple in their cloaks. Looking closer in the window at the neighbor in pink and on the phone sitting on the edge of her bed. I want to write an elegy but without the sadness.

From very old books, I read of things extinct, including the very old book itself. The knowledge is there to glean. Turning poems into pulp, silly to talk or write of cake, still I think of one that calls for a dozen eggs when I should be talking of paper and print, or talking to plush teddy bears strapped to the grills of garbage trucks or growing a Tree of Light.

III

White bridled horse on hind legs
Baby head with blue eyes
Torso in overalls
Pink rocket with a dirty nose
These are what I gathered, but they are not the ingredients for
making fire.

The half booth barely shelters. Cup and spoon lay inside the hood.
The receiver, beaten to pieces, dangles. Once wooden doors pulled
shut, like a wall crypt pulled tight for privacy: an obscene notion,
I hear everyone's keystrokes.

I fear the full bag of bedclothes on the stoop
Mattress against garbage barrels, blue and upright

I fear the briefcase abandoned on the street, yet trace the embossed
dates in metal, circa 1970s. Open the lid softly, and follow the cloth
cord to an ancient tube. Carefully. The nearby floppy disks brush my
hand. Touching the apparatus with a cloth and poking it with a stick.
Who or what is this time traveler?

What is a cathode ray?
Radiation or inert gas?
Retired or active chemicals?
The makings of television or Armageddon?

I am afraid of the cosmic ray let loose on the street (afraid of x-rays
specs or machines that see through the bone). Panic travels through
the blood as easily as aspirin.

The feather this afternoon is a black and grey tongue pointing east. The pay phone, a portal through which voices connect in sometimes pleasing ways. The hood of the half booth as private as a homemade sex tape.

I, the relic on the street, born during the time of paper and print; my replacements, attached to wireless networks, ride herd down the sidewalk

Holding close, slowing down to read the sign in the booth, tear off a tab of "I will post your flyers"

University bus drives by, sadness ensues

My days are spooked by the rotary ringtone of a cell phone ghosting a black enamel phone, heavy, and tethered to earth: that is a desk, that is gravity. In airport corridors clusters of laptops and pay phones await flight. A stranger no longer taps on the glass. To open the folding door of the booth is to enter into a cabinet of curiosities, a carnival wagon. The rotary dial is a greased wheel of chance.

Feathers are bits of bird. Eggs, an afterthought for this observer.

Once the neighbors played a recording of falling coins or stuck a pin into the receiver for free calls. This was in the past, although that is clear, I say it for myself before the time caught in the mirror turns amber.

Entering the carny wagon of childhood games: nickel pitch, shooting gallery, balloon darts, cranes/diggers, weight and age barkers. I prize gun-shaped cigarette lighters, girlie cards, switchblade combs, and stuffed bears. I do not prize plastic poodles. Now, I prize grainy vintage porn and airbrushed nudie calendars, or I return to the flea market to gaze at a portrait of a bored couple in the 1920s posing with a headstone or to rifle through a Chinese tea box full of loose sequins in rotting paper or to ponder a Buddha head or shreds of Nepali armor, or a Weimar Republic glossy of nightclub performers or a journal in English and Arabic. Translations of homilies. I bid on these tatters.

Separated coffee and milk at peace inside the cup on the street. Hard core cooing, brooding, in the back of the railroad apartment. White wings spread behind the locust tree.

Cup in the booth, finger streaks of Irish Rose on the walls.

Tintype of man with hand on his heart. My other hand is on the daguerreotypes, my eyes on a cloth monkey dressed in a suit and tie.

The cup on top of the time machine makes a composition; What is a receiver? A cradle? What is "return?" The coin slot is a finger dip into the dark.

Where are the cool blue mint hoods of Brazil?

Coffee cups brace the sides
Drunk pisses enough to drown the flame
No one touches without tissue

"Mary had a little lamb," were the first words.
The silver of the daguerreotype serves as my mirror. I'm building a time machine made from parts of the past, for when I might return through an old memory stored in wood.

I can get at the drawings or language of making things: instruction manuals for building fires or cookbooks for explosives or poisons. I have found out why we stand tall and who the commanders of the great ships are. I have learned the story of the microscope and of birds which dress in blue and purple, of how to read a sea shell. I have read of monsters of the land and sky, from the crumbles of a 19th-century text. I commit to memory views from penny postcards of sights I've never seen and actions I never witnessed—like the great swans of Long Island in the wild, or the skyline of Manhattan as seen from the deck of a paddlewheel steamer. I am impressed by cancelled postcards from the plains of a sod house or from a museum of corn.

IV

Today I opened a very old book that told of how to make matchsticks
Let me tell you about the first time I was allowed to make fire

How many rooms in the mud dauber's house?
How many pecans in the squirrel cache?
"Where did that fucking dog go?"
Asked a country neighbor in the morning.

Wooden plow marooned in the hayloft
Other tools landed and silent
The paper casings tell of metamorphosis

Into the story of the disassembled house, add handwritten figures on
cigarettes and candy cartons stored inside bread wrappers, add a meat
grinder nailed to a board and barn swallows hand-perched on a wire,
add a fireplace mantel, and the front door with its full bust of glass, and
a hope chest torn to pieces.

Putting down the neighbor's dog for the butterfly bite on my leg, I fear
the execution of the dog next door.

Taken apart, no walls only an outline of what were doors and panels.
The porch's white painted one. Stack of windows looking down on
smothered grass. The doors leaning on the wall are dangerously idle.

Portals, without purpose, hold murder views

Objects in the grass or in the barn, my father's shelter, are altered by
cold and heat. Standing in the hayloft, looking up at pulleys on the
ceiling. The carriageway welcomes black buggies, horse hair spills
out of rotted leather seats. A toy cash register lies on its side. A couch
posed on stilts, yet exposed to weather: the upholstery as thin as the
parchment skin of a Mexico City mummy dressed in the finery of grave
clothes. The death grimace of the barn cat will not lie flat between
pages.

Quilt blocks from an auction
Stranger's clothes
Not even our own threads
Become the foundations of a family quilt

Ever inscribed or in which we are mentioned
Newsprint or programs or certificates or photographs

A bread sack of October 1970 receipts: Drink DOUBLE COLA BUNNY
BREAD YOUR FRIENDLY BAKER HOLLAND DAIRY J. ZINSMEISTER CO.
FEDERAL PRODUCE UNCLE CHARLIE'S tender 'n juicy meats "YOUR
MEAT SPECIALIST" FIRST ROYAL CROWN BOTTLING DERR'S INC.
MANUFACTURERS & JOBBERS ICE SODA FOUNTAIN SUPPLIES ALL KINDS
PAPER GOODS

I, ephemera, carrying my chemical burden
I, ephemera, once paper becoming plastic becoming digital or
I, ephemera, holding the space
I, ephemera, hold the space

When I awaken
The objects of the gaze develop

Stereopticon's double image
After a night of paper and print

Under lamp, oil or wax light
Breaking the silence

Tearing at it like a child or pulling slowly at the corner
The new day dissolving like an egg in vinegar

I lie like Mother Cabrini in her glass coffin
A step ahead of mass extinction.

v

Going inside the tatters, the threads and grasses
A nest, all the elements assembled

Pixie sticks and Lincoln logs
Bonnets and cloaks

The object to be reassembled with the saved elements
Under the dust the front door waits to be opened again.

If I were a ghost, and I could be one turning the key for the thousandth
time, walking through the doorway and turning on a tap. I have heard
that ghosts are very tired, having no bloody heart they draw energy
from grids or from the living making cold spots, the cold makes me
sluggish too. I am concerned about eternal life of ghosts because most
ghosts request our silence.

In taking apart a system
A murder or a flower
To see how it works
I am not careful

I force the relationship between parts. My father could reason it out,
he had a talent for spatial arrangements. My brother could take apart a
machine but there it would lie gutted until the parts decayed and like
my brother, I could never reassemble the machine again through my
own neglect and lack of talent for seeing and understanding the nature
of physical objects.

I have no name for what is inside me that is not nature
For these metal and plastic shavings.

Toy robot with twin guns blazing. Black and embossed with science
fiction trimmings. Bright fire of the guns that go a-rat-a-tat-tat.
Tin body held together with folded metal tabs, hard robot shell makes
a machine I would not fuck with.

The day is a thin wire fence that corrals a herd of thoughts
The phrase "moving between the trailers" comes to me. Shape-shifting
very dark being pacing the lengths.

Cat army lives in the corn
Turkey buzzard takes his time almost to the nose of the car

I am alive in the trailer in the meadow packed high behind heavy
curtains. My brother's is filled with a television mostly. Kittens lived
inside the couch. Behind the door and under the tarp, no secrets, only
television.

Pile it here. Outdoors is where no one goes without a dog for fear of
the woods, of the backwaters, fear of the bridge (it might lead the way
out), fear of mirrors, of seeing one's self in the natural light after years
behind curtains.

The page is a trailer on wheels and my pen moves with it to back roads where skinned deer are dumped. The remains on the path are very dead and silvery. Bones exposed, six footsteps long and a palm wide.

A floppy disk stores my pain.

Cathedral ceilings, whirlpool baths, television and game room built into the walls. No hard copies, but a digital library of games & clothes mildewed in the dryer.

I return to the very old book unearthed from beneath the trailer floor. On marbled paper I read of a wooly mammoth dug up from a farmer's field and of one found in a block of ice with fresh greens in mouth, wearing a coat of long reddish hair and later served as meat to dogs.

Bird species are told by their markings
Bar under an eye or tail feathers

The trailer, a bookmark that replaced a farmhouse. Marbled covers,
red-edged pages. Men in hats touch the spines all around. Others
underfoot further flatten and tear.

Cursed
Underlined and argued
Agreed bright yellow or pink

I cannot describe in bird or insect song what happened to the returning soldier in the double-wide next door, a container that pours out cannon fodder

Fantasy van rocks in the night——sequins of metal and plastic spin——
—— Ferris wheel unspools

The bones of a house —— long radiator guts ——— dry on the lawn

VI

Threading raw film on a reel in the dark. When did a soldier become
a troop? Threading while riding through the House of Fear. The cart
whips through the canvas gates of Hell, torn tarp lets the light in. Swat
teams in coordinated gear. Mechanical monsters, made of rubber
masks, rags and gears, reach out from a mile away.

In my hands the image as fragile as a baby's future

I open the door slowly to let crap tumble and shut it quickly to keep
the animals inside, not sure of what can be salvaged from the lab next
door. My family says "Junk it all."

Dark smoke of the burn barrel curls in the air

I hunch over to shield the unmade in a basement room of chemical
baths and lenses. Guided by other senses, the image not yet fixed
in my hands, a spool of memory, subject to destruction by light

In the dim, I lay a saucer on an unexposed paper and
by the morning appears a circle in light brown that will darken
over time

I do it all by railroad light
Magic lanterns and carny sideshows

Eight-by-ten glossies
Bathe in the soda cooler

Dark fires of the lab's debris
Bobcat roadkill and Wild Turkey in fighting poses
Lincoln in the act of splitting a rail
Chain of chain stores
Each holding their space on a coat of arms

Certain images fixed on black paper and held by silver corners
a pileup of futures already determined in pink satin liners.

Animal-teethed Keystone View cards—double images balance
on——the wooden slide of the stereopticon

"Sea of Wool-Lambs for all the Marys Sheep Industry, Montana" 1904

"The Funeral of President McKinley—Tribute of Columbia
Commandery" 1901 noted "as solid mass of mourning."

"First Step in Pocket Book Industry, Alligators—Palm Beach Florida"
1905

Guardians of expired grammar books, a grandmother's bones hold up
the farmhouse ——— arches of a Quonset hut sway in the wind

A rescue that comes too late is not a rescue, but a salvaging of the
tatters

Patched roof and warren of drug den next door

The lab in the car trunk moving down the blacktop—— combustion
in a coffee pot ——— of batteries and pills ——— crushing black
walnuts in a vise or under a hammer for such little meat and chewed
papers shaped into a nest.

BRADLEY ROLAND WILL, 1970–2006

Everyone kept telling me I should leave town or go into hiding. I
was lost but something was holding me there. There was an image I
couldn't get out of my mind. A thin woman curled up fetal and broken,
lying in a short pool of water at the bottom of a well. I was haunted.
— from "Fragments of a Shattered Hope," Brad Will's dispatch from
Goiania, Brazil, February 2005

Most of the accounts of Brad's life list him as an anarchist, activist,
Indymedia reporter, freight-train hopper, forest defender, squatter,
fire-eater, and poet. Although Brad published very little poetry, he kept
journals of poems and ballads.

I don't know how or why, but in the early '90s Brad found his way
to Boulder, Colorado, and to the Naropa Institute (now the Naropa
University), where he became an honorary student receiving beat
transmission from Allen Ginsberg, Anne Waldman, Peter Lamborn
Wilson, and other faculty. He made lasting friends with emerging poets
on the scene such as myself, Eleni Sikelianos, and Akilah Oliver.

His legacy as a superhero among anarchists began when he came
to the East Village in 1995 and found a place in the 5th Street Squat.
When that building was demolished by the city after a fire, he famously
broke into the squat to rescue pets and other belongings, and made it
out seconds after the first wrecking ball hit. On Wall Street, he pranked
bankers by handing out bloody (red-inked) dollar bills, and sometimes

he chained himself to trees to defend New York City's community gardens. "Hey Kids, Stay in Trouble," was one of his regular sign-offs. He was involved in Steal This Radio, a pirate radio station in the neighborhood, and broadcast a live poetry show from a hidden studio where he mixed whale sounds and poetry with Bernadette Mayer or played ballads with the poet John Wright, his close friend from Naropa days.

Poetry remained his love, and on the last New Year's Day of his life, around midnight at the Poetry Project's annual marathon reading, he read this poem:

HAUNTED

There was a woman
I am trying to forget
An image
Slender hands turning the leaves in a garden
Looking for squash
An image
Wiping dirt away from beneath her son's eyes
An image
Gripping the door and tugging to make it forced shut
I wish I could forget
Haunted by her embrace
Her bones reverberate with the bulldozer's growl
She is in the dark
Waiting for a reprieve
For a strange wind to change the sky
For the earth to shift and to open

Beneath the broken bricks
Beneath the twisted pieces of steel
Beneath the fragments of a dream
In the short pool of water
She is snapped between stones
Curled fetal not hiding but waiting
For the last breath of light
The last moments of sunset
To kiss her broken face and be reborn
And finally to say
Goodnight.

Brad saw journalism as a means to achieve social justice by giving
a voice to oppressed and marginalized people, so he shot footage
of grassroots social justice movements in Latin America, which he
planned to edit into a documentary. He was very excited when Evo
Morales was elected president of Bolivia. He was also torn between
spending Christmas with his family or returning to Bolivia, where
he had been staying with indigenous communities, to witness the
inauguration of Latin America's first native president. Photographs
from his birthday party that summer show, behind his glasses, a
weariness in Brad's eyes—but also humor and gentleness.

Brad's "The Last Dispatch," his eyewitness account of the
events that were unfolding in Oaxaca, Mexico, shortly before his
murder, can readily be found online. Although his camera was rolling
when he was shot, and two arrests have been made in the past eight
years, responsibility for his murder has remained controversial. As
I write, his family and friends still seek answers from the Mexican
government.

For a long time, I thought Brad was just the poet's hero, but I soon found out he was everyone's hero. His death was mourned globally—in New Zealand, South America, and Europe. European newspapers compared his fallen image to Christ's. Subcomandante Marcos, the Zapatista leader, called Brad a kindred spirit, a friend of the people.

ACKNOWLEDGMENTS

I am grateful to the Millay Colony for the Arts, Lower Manhattan Cultural Council, and the Emily Harvey Foundation for their generous gifts of time and space.

Some excerpts of these poems have appeared in *Volt*, *1913*, *Brooklyn Rail*, *Cousin Corrine*, *Denver Quarterly*, *Mixed Blood*, and the Elena Herzog catalog from the Daum Museum of Contemporary Art.

My deepest thanks to the family of Bradley Roland Will for their permission to quote from Brad's writing. My thanks to Atticus Fierman, Robert McDaniel, Eleni Sikelianos, Marcella Durand, Elena Herzog, Portia Munson, Helen Mitsios, and Lynn Behrendt for lending their eyes and ears.

ABOUT THE AUTHOR

Brenda Coultas is the author of *The Marvelous Bones of Time* (2008) and *A Handmade Museum* (2003), which won the Norma Farber Award from the Poetry Society of America, and a Greenwall Fund publishing grant from the Academy of American Poets. She has received a New York Foundation for the Arts fellowship and a Lower Manhattan Cultural Council residency. Her poetry can be found in *The Brooklyn Rail*, *Witness*, and *Court Green*. In 2012, she completed an artist's residency at the Emily Harvey Foundation in Venice, Italy, and at the Millay Colony in Austerliz, New York. She teaches at Touro College in New York City.